Proceed to Check Out

PHOENIX POETS

ALAN SHAPIRO

Proceed to Check Out

THE UNIVERSITY OF CHICAGO PRESS

Chicago and London

The University of Chicago Press, Chicago 60637
The University of Chicago Press, Ltd., London
© 2022 by The University of Chicago
Published 2022
Printed in the United States of America

31 30 29 28 27 26 25 24 23 22   1 2 3 4 5

ISBN-13: 978-0-226-81754-5 (paper)
ISBN-13: 978-0-226-81755-2 (e-book)
DOI: https://doi.org/10.7208/chicago/9780226817552.001.0001

Library of Congress Cataloging-in-Publication Data

Names: Shapiro, Alan, 1952– author.
Title: Proceed to check out / Alan Shapiro.
Other titles: Phoenix poets.
Description: Chicago : University of Chicago Press, 2022. | Series:
    Phoenix poets
Identifiers: LCCN 2021021867 | ISBN 9780226817545 (paperback) |
    ISBN 9780226817552 (ebook)
Subjects: LCGFT: Poetry.
Classification: LCC PS3569.H338 P76 2022 | DDC 811/.54—dc23
LC record available at https://lccn.loc.gov/2021021867

♾ This paper meets the requirements of ANSI/NISO Z39.48-1992
(Permanence of Paper).

for JASON SOMMER

"Say that my glory was I had such friends."

CONTENTS

ACKNOWLEDGMENTS

The author wishes to thank the following publications in which these poems or versions of them first appeared:

> *At Length*: "Money"
> *Battery Journal*: "Pumice," "Ding Dong, the Bells Are Gonna Chime," and "Death of Alan"
> *Café Review*: "What the End Was Like" and "Art According to Curly"
> *Literary Imagination*: "Reunion in Heaven" and "The Periodic Table"
> *Literary Matters*: "Wedding Tent" and "An Arrangement"
> *New Ohio Review*: "The Great Closer" and "Hole in One"
> *Plume*: "Letters," "At the Museum of Life and Science," and "Divorce Party Bonfire"
> *Southern Cultures*: "Space Blanket"
> *Threepenny Review*: "Zoom" and "Sugar Shack"
> *Upstreet*: "Uncle Hy"

One

HOLDING CELL

1. An orangey LG dimness filled the cell like graded mist your body, as on a continuum of nothing to not-quite-something, was the densest bandwidth of.

2. The padded walls of the cell were so absolutely soundproof you could feel pressing up behind them all the ambient noise they wouldn't let you hear.

3. We can neither confirm nor deny that you had never felt so safe. That was the problem. Behind the padded walls lab-coated protocols patrolled the halls and stairwells. Embedded teams, encrypted units, viral packs, and gangs surveilled preemptively from floor to floor like white cells in a paranoid immune system flushing out what wasn't there so that it couldn't be.

4. We can neither confirm nor deny your childhood or that story in which Daddy orders the dentist not to give the boy you were a shot of lidocaine, or how the drill drills down through enamel to the very burning bottom of the nerve, for your own good, because it hurts him more than it hurts you: what we can say unequivocally is that it didn't, and it wasn't.

5. While happily you drifted in the neural void of a condemned facility, in a synaptic gap made from dendritic dead ends, axonal cul-de-sacs, messages everywhere but where you were were being fired at the speed of light, from ward to ward, and

out into the night via phone lines, satellites, and fiber optic cables buried under earth and ocean; determinations as to what to do with you went everywhere; each decision, though uncoerced, had no idea it had already been decided long before you were the object it now decided on.

6. And yet was anything you thought or did as insane as the hidden-away bricked-in Babel storage vaults of data crammed full yet exponentially expanding to the size of cities stacked on cities everybody calls the cloud?

7. On their own, in the LG nonlight, your thumbs typed on an absent keypad while you stared down into the empty screen space between them at the message they by habit sent to whom by habit waited for the bubble's flickering ellipsis to become the words that would become the words another bubble flickering in the empty screen space between your thumbs kept promising, in return, were on their way.

8. You dreamed you were a selfie taken of yourself inside the cell. You posted it, and on the one hand it received a thousand likes,

9. And on the other you were immediately notified by all your friends that they no longer wanted to be friends with anyone they didn't know. With algorithmic certainty, you understood, your thumbs typed "Totes!" in the reply box and hit Send.

10. The data records everything, prevents nothing.

11. What the data fails to prevent justifies the collecting of more data.

12. We can neither confirm nor deny that thinking nobody is watching you is just as paranoid as thinking everybody is.

13. During the evacuation, while wildfires swept down from the hills, the cell pinged with notifications from the 24/7 home security system livestreaming from the living room as camera flipped to camera from the shining standing lamp arced over the recliner to the blue light of the aquarium where goldfish circling through it flickered greenly across the room reflected in the picture window full of thrashing branches wicked with flame that blackened on the glass before imploding, and one by one the cameras room to room went black while the smoke alarm shrieked as it was meant to, loud at first, then soft and softer, intermittently, until it stopped.

14. We can neither confirm nor deny that there is an inkling of an itch beginning on your shoulder blade just below where you can reach. At first, it asks politely to be scratched. But you ignore it. Because inside the cell there's nothing else to do, you try to test your self-control. It asks again, this time a little louder, not so politely, but you don't move, you pretend you're waiting for another incoming text on your nonexistent phone; the itch insists you pay attention, it commands attention, your skin burns with the attention you refuse to give it. Unbearable the itching, your fingers the skin of your entire body itchy with the urge to scratch it, but you don't, you won't, you think by now it's not about you. It was never about you. What's at stake (we can neither confirm nor deny) is the survival of a will, of an idea of freedom; your dignity as an independent person depends on your not putting down the protean screen that isn't even there, on clinging to it while it shape-shifts into images

of balms, of soothing ointments, of lotions, which, if you order now, will come at no additional cost with a metal back scratcher that can scratch all the inaccessible places on your person that you on your own have never reached.

ZOOM

In the hospice where you died, a lot of money
was spent to make the place conform to someone's
algorithm of a home—shag-carpeted lobby,
wood-paneled elevator, particle-board furniture
with shrink-wrap thin mahogany veneer, faux-marble
linoleum tiles. There were paintings of chickens
in a barnyard on the walls of every room.
The homier they made it, the more clinical it felt.
You of course were out of it by then, the ersatz hominess
was for the living, not the almost dead.
And on the rare occasions when you woke
and tried to talk, I could only hear enough
of what you murmured to know how far away
you were from anything I knew, alone
in a remoteness that today seems almost
familiar, though no less remote, like hospice,

you might say, by another name: my face
isolated, in a square stacked with the squares
of friends and family inside the screen-sized square
our separate boxes make together, boxes
talking box to box, as in a bar or restaurant
face to face, as in a pre-posthumous world
of host and game-show faces mummified
to paste, to pasty smiles of dead celebrities
still quipping, "How many balls on a pool table?"

"Depends on how many men are playing pool!"
I think I hear you in our edgy laughter,
as if we'd won a one-way ticket to
a last resort, a Club Med of an island
rendezvous, a hidden, herded, hoard
of "I" germs doing anything to keep
alive and still be seen and heard. Funny
how signing off, no matter who I wave to,
it's you I always see wave back at me,
the two of us together once again
in a lost dimension, as if we're both on ship
and shore, stranded departing, waving till
the square goes mute and blackens, and the room
with just myself inside it feels so unreal
I'm virtually nowhere, where you are.

REUNION IN HEAVEN

I'd begin by pointing out how

in the first place there had never been a "union"

to "re,"

      to which one of them would probably

repeat how everything

I ever wrote about them,

every bit of it,

          was wrong.

And the other would agree,

          and both

would be surprised to find themselves,

for once, on the same page.

          In which case

I might tell them,

"Well, then,

                    it was good for something,"

a quip they'd just talk over:

how it wasn't just

that my account was wrong—

no, what galled them,

                    what even now

they can't forgive, isn't just that it was

riddled with mistakes,

                    but that the mistakes

themselves were riddled

with bad faith

whose purpose was to make

my bad seem better

by exaggerating theirs.

To which I'd likely say, "But

now that our bodies are behind us,

                    let's put

our so-called

          heads together

and think this through."

"Okay," I'd say, "I get it,

               there were too many of us

and not enough of you."

And when you add to that what it was like

to be small and helpless,

at the mercy

of grown-up bodies

            full of flaws

you can't not need

for everything,

how could the never-balanced

                              book

of competing burdens

                    not be cooked?

By which time I'm certain

the airy configuration

of our heads and shoulders would have shrugged or

drifted off toward airier dimensions

or simply merged

                    into entire

facelessness,

               as if to say,

no matter how you cut it,

this is not the time or place;

we'd rather not discuss it;

you should have thought of that before.

THE PERIODIC TABLE

My time around that table in that house was longer than anywhere
else I've ever been, including around that table in that house—

I have had to dig through nettle, tar, sediment, and strata; to
ancestral char, chemical traces of mere slaughter mistaken for
sacrifice; to the stone navel, the cold mineral residues of safety
in the emptiest of spaces; between rooms, on the lithic staircase
between floors where no one is now when I reach it, the dark
underworld of hallway whose abysm of dead calm made the kitchen
it led to seem livelier than it ever was, so the kitchen fixture as
you entered on a good day brightened only a little, and on a bad
intensified to surgical glare above an operating table, which was the
kidney shaped Formica table all of the elemental reckonings took
place around—

let me remind you: *then* was not wanting to be there; *now* is not
having anywhere else to go—

all weather was inside and preemptive—

forecast of spills in the spotless tabletop, of flash floods and
mudslides in the scrubbed-raw sheen—my child face the only cloud
smudge in that inverted sky I'm always looking up out of, at me, at
my old face looking down, godlike, a god I would have prayed to
if I thought that I existed or, if I had existed, could have heard the
prayer or, if I'd heard it, could have done anything to help—

somebody please tell the child nobody was "bowing it higher and higher"—there never was an "ancient floor, footworn and hollowed and thin," and remind him where the dead feet did walk in, as the timer ticked, and heat rose inside the pressure cooker where the cow tongue cooked, each tick unbearable relief from the silent interval through which from tick to tick he plummeted till the vent sprung open and began to whistle with the rising steam—

would somebody please tell the child he doesn't have to eat the boiled tongue—

nobody's there to make him; for goodness' sake there isn't even a child

and it was never the home where when you had to go there they had to take you in but the one whose sounds and sweet airs that give delight and hurt not were only audible from somewhere else so that you had to go away to hear them, which is how they drew you back, and why, drawn back, you couldn't bear to stay—

because what did not delight did hurt—

and even the scrubbed body was filthy, filthy, filthy—hey! what crawled up inside of you and died?

how could I not invent this sorry power: holding back; not doing; not saying—my hiding place (wherever I was) inside my body—where I could think anything, and did, and no one was the wiser—where I got away with murder—and everyone but me died every day.

Now everyone but me is dead.

Shame on me.

SPACE BLANKET

If in the crinkling thin-as-air metallic
blankets there are flashes signaling back
and forth over the little bodies wrapped
inside them sleeping on cage floor, gym floor,

floor of a defunct warehouse, don't think of torch
fires, beacons of distress, or in the softness
any sign of soothing, though they're soft
as tissue, even softer, yet untearable,

a just-as-tough-as-soft parental foil
no cold can cool or heat can burn. Weightless,
bulkless, and even though the largest swath
can fold into the smallest sack, don't think

efficiency or comfort, or even of
the children sleeping uncomfortably in bulk
alone behind bars in detention centers;
instead, imagine you are sleeping in it too,

your body, you, like a spaceship pushing up
through thinning atmospheres of friction, sealed
in a material that neither cools nor warms
what otherwise would only freeze or fry:

imagine it surviving, nothing else,
hurtling on through nowhere, holding nothing,
like foil wrapped up in leftovers of foil
inside the unplugged fridge of outer space.

THE GREAT CLOSER

How the great closer—when the batter lunged
and swung through the curve for strike three—
turned his back to the plate as if there were no batter,
and his one concession to the moment
(that there even was a moment) was
to hitch one shoulder as if to shrug off
a slight annoyance, while his face, unbothered
by expression, measured its mastery by what
it wouldn't feel, or show, was like and not like us,
our faces, lips, how, when I tried to kiss yours,
they shut tight against what up to then, it seemed,
they'd opened to so eagerly I never thought
they ever wouldn't or imagined you might ever
turn away, not just as if I wasn't there but
never had been. And weren't we, maybe, like
the batter too, and not, the way he flipped the bat and
caught it and as he strolled back to the dugout,
holding the bat up, seemed to study it
with such rabbinical amazement
you could almost think he'd failed on purpose
so he could finally see within the bat
whatever lack the bat, not knowing it was lacking,
had hidden in the grain to show him now?

UNCLE HY

I.

I never knew why or how his doctor's bag ended up on a shelf in a side room of our cellar—in so remote a corner whoever put it there must not have wanted anyone to ever find it. When I discovered it, exploring the netherworld of what I lived above, it looked exotically Methuselian, like the kind of bag Old Doc Adams on *Gunsmoke* carried with him through the dust-hazy streets of Dodge, its brown leather fissured like alligator skin with a loose leather handle to which a tiny key was tied. It fit the lock on the bronze buckle, and the bag, which was rounded at the top when it was closed, became balky, rectangular when the key turned and the bag snapped open. A centipede crawled out. A chilly odor, medicinal and stale, rose from the dark inside it. At the bottom lay a tray of empty slots and small compartments; in a large side pocket I found a pair of tweezers, a tiny bottle of iodine, the lens of a magnifying glass without the frame, a packet of bandages, and a tongue depressor that, slipped from its crinkly package, looked like the stick part of a popsicle. From the pocket opposite, I pulled out a stethoscope whose ear tips had been snapped or cut off and whose chest piece was cracked, so when I tried to listen to my heart the way Doc Adams did whenever someone on the show was shot or sick, moving the chest piece over chest and stomach while saying kindly, "Take a deep breath, son, now out, now in, again, again," no sound but my own voice came through the tubing.

2.

I was a baby when Uncle Hy was diagnosed with lung cancer—three months later he was dead. There was one picture taken of him just after the war on the mantelpiece above our unused fireplace; he's at the beach, and his toddler son Jeffrey wearing a white sailor hat is in his lap. The camera catches Jeffrey squirming in Hy's arm; the child's eyes shut tight, mouth grimacing, his body all rigid torque as if he's being beaten up by ghosts while Hy stares calmly, smiling at the camera, an unlit cigarette in the corner of his mouth; he's tanned, handsome—and with his trim mustache he's a dead ringer for Tyrone Power. Everyone used to say that, and such a nice guy too, salt of the earth, give you the shirt off his back, though this was offered in a tone of bafflement, as if his kindness somehow didn't add up, was the last thing you'd expect, given something else about him that they never mentioned, at least not in front of children.

A photo of a dead relative but the only ones who know are dying & they will be cleaned out & replaced by younger, more contemporary pictures

3.

I knew enough to keep the bag a secret. Upstairs and down, that house was crisscrossed with trip wires of rules, limits, prohibitions, and restrictions, many of which you didn't know about until you broke them. It was like what Dodge appeared to be at the opening of every episode—a pokey yet bustling town of quaint stagecoaches, covered wagons, and cowboys on horseback all maneuvering peacefully somehow through the one street while merchants, farmers, and corseted women with piled up hair that little hats held in place stroll up and down the wooden sidewalks past the general store, the jail, the bank, the louvered saloon doors swinging open and closed on happy drinkers, and all the while abrasions of tone and gesture, and missteps too slight to notice under everybody's

how the trees in the backyard are of a genus & species but near confessions & surreptitious conversations

maybe death will stop the obsessive criticism & something will have to take its place & then your reputation undergoes a renaissance because the new is not the old.

how little has Δ when we think of home

whether tires, shade trees forts

their descendants family members

noses, were building up past umbrage into rage, in the wake of which, in a black frock coat, brown bag in hand, Old Doc Adams would come running.

4.

The day I find the bag, Hy has been long dead, and Jeffrey, whom I've never met, is grown and living in a halfway house for troubled men. I'm standing on a chair with the bag open beside me. I'm about to operate; my patient is the centipede I've picked up with the tweezers and am now holding up to examine under the dim bulb hanging from the ceiling. He's not from around here, is he, no, he's a drifter, maybe a rustler, maybe a gunslinger, a bad hombre in other words, but it's not my place to judge. I'm just a doctor. And he's been shot—I can tell he's hurt bad by how still he is, only the tiny pincers waving back and forth. "Tell me your name son," I say. "Okay Horace, now you rest easy. The bullet's gone plumb through your belly, I'm going to have to clean the wound before the germs get in." He rolls up in a ball when I place him on the table, so with the tongue depressor I wedge him open and squeeze a drop of iodine onto his underside, and in the magnifying glass I watch the little segments of him quiver and buckle as the ointment spreads. I want to dab him with a gauze pad, but when I remove the tongue depressor, he curls up even tighter. I gently place the chest piece of the stethoscope on top of him and listen. No breath. No heartbeat. A goner. I want to feel something for him, but the room is full of the maimed and wounded. So I find another injured soul and get to work.

5.

They're all goners now, everyone who knew my uncle's story, including Jeffrey, who drifted from halfway house to institution

back to halfway house until the mid-seventies when he jumped
to his death from a bedroom window. The story exists only in
fragments I gleaned as a child by stealth and accident, from
whispered hints and innuendos, snatches of kitchen gossip heard
from hallways, someone talking on another line when I'd pick up
a phone, or overheard at night from the back seat of the car when
they thought I was sleeping—it had something to do with what Hy
saw overseas as a medic in the war, an island harbor clogged with
bodies floating facedown, something about a pile of burning boots,
teeth drilled without lidocaine for the fun of it, and after all that to
come home to a child like that, a child no one could handle, who
was never right in the head, not really, even before Hy returned,
even if after he returned the child got so much worse. Still, imagine
having to come home to that.

6.

Some miraculous change took place at death. Until you died
you should have known better. Until you died you got what you
deserved. You were your own fault. And the unforgiving stories
people told behind your back, which you deciphered from their
every gesture, look, and intonation—that was how they let you
know just who you were and where you stood in the big picture and
what needed fixing and how it was all up to you to fix it, though
poor fuck that you were you never would. But once you died it was
your story, not you, that needed fixing. And it was their job to fix
it. Because they knew, they all knew, consciously or not, what they
had done and were still doing to their own children; they knew
(even the worst of them) exactly who they were. By gossiping about
each other they could reassure themselves they weren't that bad. But
once you died you became their plea for mercy. They doctored you
into the person they hoped they'd be themselves in the stories told

about them when they died. The screwups that, while you lived, proved you had no one but yourself to blame now proved, once you were gone, how bad your luck was, how, damn it, you just could never catch a break. Because everyone would someday need Doc Adams, everyone became Doc Adams to your busted soul.

7.

Because God knew, if no one else did, what it cost them to prepare you for the world that lay in wait for you beyond the safety of your father's house, a world of Nazi-bastards, and goyish boss men who despite their glad-handing would always see you as the dirty Jew you were. Only God knew how the fathers hated themselves for what they knew they'd do again over and over even while they promised not to, how the smack of the closed fist went on echoing inside them long into the night. Only God knew the chilly marriage bed, the ends not made to meet, the chewed-on during silent meals. Day after goddamn day the universe expanded to make room for everything only God could know.

8.

There's too much damage for one old country doctor in a frontier town, in a single episode of a single season. The patients pile up, and the plot falters without thickening. Me, Doc Adams stops asking for names. Me, Doc Adams stops wondering about anybody's story. Me, Doc Adams works mechanically without thinking to fill the tray of slots and compartments with dead roly-polies, centipedes, black ants, brown ants, flies, and spiders, which he tells himself he's sending to the lab for further study even while he knows he's just plumb done with medicine: he closes up the bag, he locks it, returns it to the shelf, and leaves it there safe in the dark where it belongs, where it can do no harm.

PUMICE

Not slaughterhouse, but abattoir, that's what he always called it.
Abattoir, from the French *abattre*, meaning to beat down with
a stick, conjoined to "oir" to signify a place where something,
anything, purposeful is done—from which we get "abate," meaning
to diminish, to lessen; a French fumigation in effect of the
Germanic meat stench clinging, unabated, to his clothes, skin, lips,
and hands no scrubbing could wash off, which he brought back
every evening to our house from what he didn't need to call a house
for us to know we lived in something like it too.

She served us moving around the table like volcanic steam that
whitens into something almost dreamlike in its calm the farther off
it spirals from the crater.

And while the rest of us were being served, you could still smell it
through the soapy fragrance of his just-washed hands that rested
fisted like mitts of pumice on the table, annoyed, impatient in their
very stillness, while the meat steamed and oil ran in tiny channels
over the charred edges, seeping pinkly into pools where meat met
plate.

Meticulously as a jeweler, he cut the meat into pieces that he then
cut into smaller pieces, then lifted each piece daintily one at a time
on one prong of the fork into his mouth.

His jaw cracked when he chewed, as if he chewed pumice.

Around the silent table the cracking jaw and the chewing carried on a conversation about the taste of pumice nobody understood or dared interrupt.

She wouldn't sit or eat till later, not till we were finished and he had taken us one by one to the bathtub for the nightly bath

where it was as if the faint smell on his hands and not his hands would wash you, yes, a little too roughly, but only a little, only to keep the smell that washed you from getting on you too. Rough, quick, and hard, they scrubbed the skin raw and kept scrubbing till they reddened from the skin the burning filth that only burning let you know was there.

Volcanic rock explodes as liquid from unimaginable heat and pressure—and in the moment of explosion the super heat of the rock is supercooled by air so swiftly that the bubbles of gas inside it that the heat releases freeze in the releasing, in the sudden loss of heat, as in a still shot of carbonated water.

Did his hand feel cold because the water scalded, or did the water feel scalding because his hand was cold? Either way, the scalding and the cold made the skin feel scolded.

Sometimes while he turned you this way and that to reach the most reluctant places on the body (not exactly like an animal you might be readying for sacrifice), he mumbled to himself about price ceilings and regulations, inspectors, goons, and even rabbis you had to pay not to look too closely before they'd give their blessing, before they'd say the meat was clean—and yet the awful offal offered no augury, no Heed! Hark! Lo! of prophecy,

or, for that matter, profit, not for him at least,

only, as he put it, the shit

of a dog-eat-dog world not even a dog would eat,

spilled out from slit carcass onto plant floor, shoveled and dumped

steaming into the Charles River

until the stink of the Charles became a can't-miss sight of the city,

and the city shut the business down.

But that was later. What he expected all along. His luck. Just his
luck. In the meantime, the smell of slaughter clung to the house like
a reputation nobody could lose.

After the bath, he lay down next to us, each one in turn, me first,
the youngest, then David, then Beth, the gruff paw that finally
from all that scrubbing almost didn't smell of meat now fumbling
to caress your ear, stroking the soft whorl of it oafishly, touching,
pinching lightly the softer lobe, feeling it with a kind of disbelief,
as if astonished by the softness, how softness such as that were even
possible.

While she ate and cleaned up, drifting cloudlike far away from who
knew what now-dormant crater,

we each fell asleep with him beside us, hand on our ears, covering them, pressing down as if to keep whatever else he might have still been saying about the day behind him or the night ahead from finding some way in.

SUGAR SHACK

Nothing so clear and certain as their low somber sincere outraged voices at the kitchen table talking with the uncle about the cousin who out of the blue has up and left his wife and kids to "shack up" with some "floozy" half his age; shack up, I'm thinking, means as in a shack, but why would anyone trade in a real house for a shack unless there's something good about a floozy, something good about how bad a floozy is, which makes no sense. The only shack I know about is the crazy little sugar shack where a cute little girly is a-workin' in a black leotard, whose feet are bare, though what's so great about bare feet I couldn't tell you, or why a shack made out of wood is called a sugar shack. I am always told when it comes to sugar my eyes are bigger than my stomach. Which must be true too of the little girly because she falls in love with the singer when he puts on some trash, which she clearly considers a good thing, though in what way? Trash is what you take out, not put on. The floozy is trash too. I'm confused by the comfort in their angry voices, the sense of safety in their back and forth about the dangerous "game" the cousin's playing. The song is all I have to help me think about the story; the story is all I have to help me think about the song. My ears are bigger than my brain. Around the kitchen table the clarity plays confusion in a tug of war, the certain what of selfish, thoughtless, bad, is pulling back against the why, how could he, for what, a little tramp? There's sugar now in the look my parents look with at each other and at the uncle, a sweetness made up somehow out of soothe and seethe, out of absolute agreement about important goodnesses the tramp-floozy-trash mysteriously clarifies. It's clear you put on trash for sugar, but how can sugar or trash be like clothes, or like a record player, or like a prank, a trick? There is no safety in a shack, which must be why the girly and the singer leave it for a house, but there must be something good too about danger, something mixed up with sugar, which must be why, once they are safe inside the house, they dream about returning to the shack. This much I know, what makes a house safe: you do what you are told, no questions asked; you give no lip; you eat what food is put before you; you take out the trash; you never put it on; you throw away as shameful, selfish, no good, what in you has its own ideas. The back and forth, the going over and over— you do this, not that, think this, not that—is like a vault down in the basement of a house where all the family jewels are kept. I don't know what he means but I have learned my lesson well enough to know that when my father later tells me just remember Al they all feel the same when you're inside them, he isn't talking about vaults or houses.

MONEY

Every surface glittered as if the glittering
alone could keep all dirt from falling through
the stringent tang of cleaner in the air,
seal it away up near the ceiling fan
that knitted dark and light shapes from the smoke.

                    *

Spindle of red yarn on one side, spindle
of yellow on the other, turning, always
turning as the needles clicked continuously,
crossing over and under, looping loop
to loop down rows of an intermeshing red
and yellow never-ending chrysalis
into what I never knew, since it was always
only just beginning to emerge.

                    *

All of the wooden surfaces bright as glass
gave off a just-buffed lemony aroma
while dust motes hung like stirred-up silt in water
high overhead, as high as they could go,
as if afraid to fall back through the clarity
their absence made.

                    What no one ever spoke of
was saying itself through the little that was said,

something to do with money, which had to do
with her, head down, knitting on the couch,
with how the pink skin on the inside of
her palms and fingers ("white" as mine, which were
as pink as hers) was looped with a dark brown
called black, each one entangling the other
till each was neither, a confused and busy
flickering black and white as purple looped

through orange looped through green. His money spoke
because aside from money, he was a man
of few words. It was said he could afford to be,
since he was loaded, "filthy rich," they said.
You breathed his money in like smoke.
The glittering of all the surfaces,
the lemony aroma of the wood,
the tang of cleaner, the needles clicking, clicking—
all that would be the only explanation,
all that informed you (if you didn't know
already) in all the ways you might pretend
you didn't hear it, never listened to it,
that he could live with whomever the hell he wanted,
sleep with whomever, he didn't have to please you,
you had to please him while he sat in silence,
amused or not, contemptuous or not:
money said you couldn't say a word.

*

There was Aunt Jemima and there was her.
Aunt Jemima smiling from the pancake box,
smiling at me, her white teeth whiter than mine,

made whiter by the smile she kept on smiling,
as if I'd just said something sweet or funny;
the smile said there was nothing I could do
that wouldn't please her; the smile called me honey
chile, precious, sugar, convinced me that's all I was.
The smile said whatever I needed it to say.

But that one, that one, that one never smiled.
Never looked at me; in the not-smiling,
not-looking, I felt a baffling chill. I saw
a chilly unself I hadn't known about.
I had to hate that self, there was no other way
to keep the rest of everything around me
warm and clear as it had always been.

*

Money was a wet bar between living room
and kitchen, bottles of different sizes, different
colors, tall ones and short ones, red and gold,
amber and pink and blue ones pushed together
like a model city skyline made of bottles,
on every one of which money had drawn
a black line at the level of the liquid,
like pencil marks on the basement wall my parents
drew once a year to measure how much I'd grown.

*

I found her one time at the wet bar sink,
holding a bottle under the tap until
the amber rose back level with the line.
And when she turned to find me there, her face

without surprise flickered with no expression
I could read—I was going to write "almost
without emotion." I was going to write
"like any president's on any bill."
I was going to write "as if she half-
expected to be caught"—but whatever stitch
or snag of history bound us to this moment,
the moment made no bond between us. Even while
she raised one finger slowly to her lips
and smiled, her smile said, don't think for a second
this is "our little secret":
It isn't little. And there is no "our."

*

Because I was too dumb, too green to know
there was a war on, and the child I was
was also enemy combatant—forever
blundering into zones of no return
that she, fixed, knitting, head down, on the couch,
already occupied, between the spindles
while the needles ticking like a time bomb
said, get out of here, get out. Get out.

*

The muffled clicking, the spindles turning, the ash-
trays filling up with stubbed-out rubble from which
smoke spindled upward, driven by the sprayed,
the buffed, the scrubbed clean, how the small talk stitched
itself around the filthy richness of
the old man's silence no one could say a word
about until the car ride home, and did

you notice how she never lifted a finger,
didn't so much as clear the table, wash
a dish, a regular queen of Sheba that one,
that one that one, not to be believed;
all the way home it filled the car, the second-
hand smoke of sovereignty and self-abasement
tangling all together into a cloud
I couldn't not inhale, that couldn't not
keep tangling into purl stitch, seed stitch, garter
and cross so deeply, tightly through me through
those afternoons it left no trace of seam
to see it by, no loop come loose enough
to loosen, no fray to show me what I was.

                            *

Except as phantom of what money does,
the phantom of a phantom, when he died, she vanished
doubly into never having been.

                            *

                            Then it's ten years later,
I'm a college boy, a summer taxi driver,
my landlords are a mixed-race couple, Ronald,
who's Black and middle aged, a communist,
and Joy, who's white and my age, even younger,
a party member too, though mostly these days
she's home with Che, their newborn, who at the moment
is fast asleep against her chest. To them,
to all their friends, there's a war on,
the frontline's everywhere, and all of us,

left and right, are grunts caught in the toils
of an unconscious mastermind, although
right now, right here, you wouldn't know it.
We're on the front stoop of their triple-decker
in the early evening, drinking with a few neighbors,
some white, some Black, a joint is circulating.

Ronald's still in the drab gray earnest suit
he wears when he's out organizing, or canvassing,
recruiting for the party I won't join—
too many meetings, bro, I always tell him,
and he never laughs. I'm always trying
to make him laugh, to overcome his cool
resistance. I never do. Remote, aloof,
unreachably serious, it's impossible
not to feel disapproved of by his aloofness.
Joy tells me it isn't personal, that's just Ronald,
he's like that with everyone, but no, I think,
it's me, it must be me he doesn't like.
I need him to like me, I don't know why.

He's half asleep, face wet with sweat, eyes closed,
one elbow on a step, he's leaning back,
the joint between two fingers, he inhales
deeply, deeply inhales again and says
into the thick long plume he takes his time
releasing, passing me the joint, "Shit man,
only so many days like this a man can stand,"

his voice weighed down with weariness so rare
for him I hardly hear it, as if it can't
push through the smoke it's spoken in; I'm moved,
I feel confided in, I want him to know
how moved I am, "I hear you, man" I say,
then take a hit and pass the joint to Joy,
and when I turn back he is looking at me,
incredulous, and then begins to laugh,
he's laughing but, it seems, without amusement;
the laughter ripping the smoke to shreds, and all
the shreds are saying, "What? You hear me? You?
You sorry fucking little motherfucker!"

Two

RECURRING DREAMS

The see-through bubble I am driving is as close
to being outside as inside possibly could be,
a skin to airy thinness beat that's turning, going
nowhere into getting somewhere through
what isn't anywhere but just a static
vacuum red lights in the windshield
and white lights in the rearview fill
with premises of other places while
I drive in place alone in a mass transit to
the moment when the bubble breaks.

*

I'm climbing up stairs to run down a hall
to a stairwell and more stairs and more
halls in a school tall as a hospital; I'm late
for class, except I don't know where
the class is or even what it is, or how
everywhere in a thousand rooms
the same proctor says "Begin," and children—
each with name tags in assigned seats, pencils
poised above the page—look up and smile
as I run past with nothing in my hand.

*

I'm the only one around the table
I'm not sure isn't dead, though I will be soon,

I'm sure, if nothing's done, and no one's doing
anything, not my mother or father, not Beth,
not David. They just continue eating, not speaking,
heads bent avidly over plates
of nothing that every tine of every fork
lifts glittering into holes that chew and swallow,
chew and swallow, rhythmic as the pick
and shovel of a chain gang; everyone is lifting
now in sync, in silence, the dead and soon to be, alike.

*

I'm on a thin ledge halfway up a cliff
above a quarry. And though my back
is pressing hard against the cliff face,
the ledge is only wide enough
to slow the slipping. The whole time
I'm slipping but not falling, always
about to fall, forever frozen in the
early terror of the giving way's
refusal to give way to the free
fall I can't do anything to stop.

*

Eleven years after his death, on his lunch break,
in his best suit, the double-breasted gray-striped Giorgio
Armani suit he wanted to be buried in, my dad has called me
down to the hotel lobby where apropos of nothing
he says he just found out he has a younger brother,
younger than I am. And I say, "So? For this you dressed up,
you called me, to tell me this?" And he says, "Just
bring me another suit, okay, Al?" And I say, "Sure,

Dad, sure," even though by then it dawns on me that
he was cremated, not buried; there was never any suit.

*

I wake with my ex beside me,
not you, and her parents
standing beside the bed
grinning happy as thieves,
dividing up the spoils
I've become, and you,
the very thought of you
just then, is what—
if not the elsewhere
of all heat in the universe
while I lie frozen in a
permafrost of sheets?

That's when I wake, relieved
and grateful that it's you,
not her, beside me, you,
my one, my only
refuge, redoubt,
which is when
the dream cold comes
back to remind me
whatever it is I've
left behind me
I can neither retrieve
nor wake without.

*

Silence of caged pacing on the bed,
of hip bones under fur rising
and falling as it turns and turns and of a
purring I can almost hear now coming
from a place so far away inside it
that it must be roaring there so that
the less I feel like I could tame it
by lying down beside it,
the more lying down beside it is all
I think of as it paces and purrs.

*

When the cave damp darkened and narrowed
into sheer black absence, pressing like chilled forceps
at my shoulders so I couldn't push forward
or slip back, I became the way the absence woke
into the thought of what it was. And what it was
was what it wanted, only later, once it had been pulled
out, pulled through, to a bright blinding, and a voice
on the bed below it where the black cave had been
was pleading for a smoke, a drag, just one
puff, please, I'm just not ready yet.

Three

THE NET

is what gets tangled
in the net and caught;
a thinking hauled
up from what remains
unthought;

made of what is
passing through it,
what it displaces,
the thing displaced,
the empty spaces

in the mesh
that make the net
a net, a what
imagining
a who

imagining the
what it came from
to return to,
only sure
that what it shares

with everything
it isn't now
is how
it disappears—
unfixed, unfinished,

billowing with a wily
will-lessness
to stay awake,
for waking's sake,
as if all sense

of you and I
is what the
waking catches
and won't
let loose and

even passion's
not quite passion
till its absence
tangles in the net
and thrashes.

WEDDING TENT

The canvas billowed, and the guy wires swayed.

Up and down the long communal tables
first one and then another guest looked up,
stopped talking, silent for a moment, then
as if on cue, chairs falling back behind them,
everybody ran with wedding programs
held to bent heads through the downpour
through wet fields, frantic, pressing keys to find
their car among the rows of cars all flashing,
"Hey, over here! No, over here! No, here!"

The canvas flapped and billowed, and the poles bent.

The guy wires whistled with the wind that pushed
clouds into clouds whose paler edges pulsed
erratically with light so massive yet
so eerily mute it could have been itself
a violence too big for any sound.

The canvas billowed, and all outside poured in

as banners loosened and broke free and flew
like just-unshackled dragons dragging tails
over tables, toppling place names, bouquets,
wine cups and water glasses, crumpled napkins

tumbling to the grass with paper plates
the steaks had been too eaten to hold down.
And as if greater vows had only just
now been exchanged,

                    the canvas clapped, the guy
wires swayed and whistled, and the strung lights swung
over blown-over barrels spilling out
already rancid cornucopias
of trash that leaped and spun maniacally
out through the entrance like a wind-roused rabble
unready for our revels to be ended—

What did they think, the fools, we'd let them just
drive off as if there'd been no sloppy toasts
or sloppier forget-me-nots, as if
what they had set in motion wouldn't follow
right to their very doors, houses, bedrooms,
their sweetly scented undefiled sheets?

The bent poles finally broke, the guy wires snapped,

and the collapsing canvas whirled away
to join the antic fanfare of a refuse
that refused to stop, for whom the party now
was always just beginning as they leap-
frogged over one another, tumbled and shoved
and pushed on joyously through a hard rain inch
by patient inch after the flashing car
lights disappearing far across the field.

DIVORCE PARTY BONFIRE

As in a secret rite, a ceremony in a book of legends, on a winter
night they stand around a kind of pyre jerry-built from sticks and
branches forgotten storms had littered the field with, logs doused
in lighter fluid, cartons of dumped-out depositions, snapshots,
memorabilia, flammable knickknacks, talismans no longer magical,
cards, effigies, early handwritten love notes mixed with later printed
texts and emails kept as evidence of fact, of counter fact, conditional
appeasements giving way to bullet-point conditions, nonnegotiable
demands, bundles of pads of legal-size paper on which from page
to page, as in a time-lapse game of solitaire, the con columns keep
getting longer while the pros shrink.

Instead of prayers, they each in turn say something funny, or try
to, eager to prove what once was hard to swallow can be laughed
at now even if the laughter sounds less wry than rueful: "I was so
tired of being lonely, I got divorced." "Forget love 'm and leave 'm,
from now on I'm cutting straight to the division of property!" "My
ex-husband, he was such a screamer during sex, especially when I
walked in on him." Old pilgrims who have lost their way yet still
expect relief, if not rejuvenation, a great if brief unburdening, as if
they all, and not just one of them, have dragged a feather mattress
still imprinted with the ghost-weight of sleeping bodies from truck
to field to fire pit and heave-hoed it so perfectly on top it smothers
the frail, nascent flickering of match after match after match, which,

when it finally catches, brings no relief, no lightening, because the blaze gusts out everywhere at once through gaps and openings, and everybody has to step back from the sudden heat's bright sirocco into a polar night so cold it only drives them forward again from colder back to hotter back to colder, in a doleful goading, in and out of visibility, flickering on and off like herky-jerky GIFs a faulty server on a flat screen in a feedback loop keeps coughing up and swallowing.

DING DONG, THE BELLS ARE GONNA CHIME

A year after your husband's death, in the middle of my divorce, on
the way to your granddaughter's wedding, after the two long flights,
the balky wheelchair you were sure I wasn't pushing fast enough to
get us to the gate on time and almost didn't, and wouldn't that have
served me right, wouldn't that have made me happy, not to mention
the special food I forgot to order from the airline in advance, the
shitty little tin box of a rental car a good son would have spent a
little something extra on to make his mother comfortable, after all
that and then

two hours of driving in silence neither of us were in any hurry to
break, the closest thing to pleasure we could find with one another,
the flatlands giving way to hills, the hills to mountains, and though
the sky where we were was bright blue, above the mountains we
were heading up into a massive gray-green thunderhead smoldered
and flashed as if

about to blow wide open though it only kept darkening until as the
ascent steepened it spilled over the car in an avalanche of rain—

"Welcome to the country of marriage!" you announced, turning to
me, and smiled, and suddenly remarkably the chill splinters, breaks,
and we're laughing together for the first time in a long time, if only
for a moment, the freak amity catching us unawares—where had
it come from, and why now, why here, absurdly, had it found us
at the bottom of a vertical flood, all sense of road or motion gone,

the wipers blindly wiping water away from water, while we laugh together freely without derision, at least until the storm passes and the air brightens and the road is needle sharp before us in a flat line straight to where we're headed?

WHAT THE END WAS LIKE

There was howling somewhere hard to pinpoint, like a penned
mutt in a pen no bigger than a closet pacing and howling all day
every day, from all directions howling so when it sometimes did
stop, never for long (your hand again unthinkingly by habit
on my shoulder, or mine on yours), the sudden stark uneasy
quiet grew even more unbearable because we spent it listening
for the barking to return, as it would, and did, and when it didn't,
finally all the mutt would do was cower at our approach, its hackles up,
snout on paws, lips retracted slightly, trembling just enough
for us to see the fang tips, to hear the growling low and faint
and frighteningly softer than a purr. White cur of our last days,
blue ice of eyes that couldn't tell freedom from backed-into
corner, danger from offered hand, catcall from cooing
"come on now, baby, what's wrong now, baby, shhhh."

OPPORTUNITY

Your new love waited for you in the bed that had been ours, your
    face flush,
impatient to get back to him, to be with everything I wasn't,
    wouldn't be, or couldn't,

you and I one last time, face to face in the dream's doorway, night
    behind me;
chill of night between us, there in that moment as the door effaced
    us,

there was this sorrow for the un-deactivated rover I was just then in
    your eyes,
brief glitch of sympathy, if not quite love, to see me

on the red planet I had been exploring longer than anyone
    expected, stuck
in a massive crater, half buried in a dust storm but with wheels
    churning

and sensors flashing as if I hadn't realized the data I'd been
    programmed to collect,
and was still collecting even then, could now no longer be received
    or sent.

INDIFFERENCE

Not indifference, exactly, but "the semi-lust of intentional indifference"—the way, for instance, when a new text pinged on his cell phone long after midnight he didn't bother rolling over to see if it was her, even though he'd been awake, wide-eyed in the dark, unable to sleep, hoping she would call or text, and playing back their earlier conversation, during which her voice showed no evidence of missing him even while she said she did, said so somehow too perfunctorily, half-heartedly, and maybe it was only later she began to fear he'd heard it in her voice, the relief and excitement she'd been careful up to then to hide, the undertone of "honey I am happy here without you" in the tone of "of course I miss you honey." The phone pinged again and again; he didn't look in its direction; he imagined everything she'd hear inside his non-reply: that he was happy too, happier than before, or that he wasn't there or was there but with someone else already, so engrossed in her and with her he couldn't hear the feeble pinging. His silence was a wall between adjoining cells; he was tapping on the wall, a prisoner, communicating through the wall to her who like himself was listening, ear to the wall, as if there were a wall and she was there behind it and it wasn't just the silence of his bed as it went on spinning at warp speed through some wormhole leading to the farthest reaches of where he all along had only been.

FROM THE HALLWAY

Behind the door
ajar, is it
your bashfulness
or mine condensing
up the mirror
I'm imagining I am

that won't quite let
me picture the plastic
rustling of the shower
curtain sliding
open to a faint
after-shower

dripping onto
tile, onto bath
mat at wider
and fainter intervals
that tauten attention
to a caught breath

at the mere hint
of skin on towel,
where dry dampens
and wet dries, so
bashfully blurred
that I'm abashed

even as mirror
to see this much,
this near, which,
like steam on glass,
you slip, still dripping,
out of as it clears

to just a footprint
in the damp mat
I'm now free to study
frankly for the shy
feel till it fades
of toe and heel,

calf, knee,
hip, and every
twist and bend
of every posture
only absence
leaves me free

to picture, free
and sad because
you and I, it seems,
want only absence
that wants only presence
that wants only

blinding steam?

ANIMAL CRACKERS

You are a billfold
of play money
I've ponied up to buy
this see-through
blindfold with,
which I forget I'm wearing
when I see you
not look at me like that.
A silk's ear
from a pig's purse
can't make a molehill
out of a mole rat.

What I mean is
I'm the elephant in the room
I can't think outside the box of,
and you are the mother
whippersnapper
of the mother whip
I keep my wobbly balance on a ball by
before a burning hoop
I'm hot to jump through
until I do.

What I mean is, dear,
this circus is a regular zoo,
and the keepers who
have trained us have
run off
to join the circuits
of an inner
carousel they've keyed up
just for us, their one-trick
ponies going round and round
together, sliding up and down
these separate poles.

AN ARRANGEMENT

You, mornings in the white chair, bare legs draped
over chair arm, the other pillowing your back,
robe bunched up, thigh exposed, foot inching up
and down the arching instep of the other,
touching you as maybe you imagine
somebody (who? I wonder) would, or did
(how long ago, just how long has it been?),
in the right place, with the precise finesse
of pressure shifting at the pace you needed
to lift you from yourself the way heat teases
smoke signals from the cup between your hands
too far away, faint, tangled up to read.

Honey (can I call you Honey?), don't get me wrong—
this thing we don't want to be seen as doing
might be just what it is we do, have done,
can't help but keep on doing no matter what:
like pieces from two puzzles shattered long
ago, not meant to fit, yet somehow do
by happenstance, enough at least to turn
the shattering into a crazy glue
that holds us safe inside where you now get
to feel desired in the way that makes me feel
deserted in the very way I want.

So what if these broken pieces we've become
don't quite resolve into a single picture
anyone else but us would recognize
as love or like love; we at least can tell
ourselves, if not each other, that we've found
a not unintimate puzzling give and take
(not felt in other company) in which
you draw one foot so slowly up
and down the other I can almost think
you think I'm watching, or someone like me is.

BACKWARD

This Odysseus died before reaching home, that Penelope ran off
with a suitor.

You and I at this age need another story, one that's all envoi and
afterword, even before it happens.

The ancient Greeks believed we walk backward into the future,
facing the past—the way I sit with my back to the tunnel so I can
watch the bright station slide by and shrink away into the dark I'm
hurtling through.

Hey, do you ever feel like I do, like Benjamin Button in reverse, I
mean, like every second of every day you're dying normally just like
everyone else?

When I was a kid a friend and I tried sneaking into *The Ten
Commandments* by walking backward under the marquee as people
came walking out. We didn't get to see more than the coming
attraction of *Some Like It Hot* before the shriveled Moses of an
usher in his clownish fez, gold-epauletted red vest, and black bow
tie rounded us up and roughly by the ear escorted us from the
auditorium. He called us hoodlums, fancy-pants gangsters. His
voice is the voice I imagine hearing just after I die.

Sometimes I feel like I have lived my entire life out of a suitcase but
not gone anywhere.

It's like I'm not aware I'm wearing this virtual reality headset of a long-ago present where I never was, so I can think I am.

It's like an eternal return minus the returning.

That sense that I'm walking backward toward someone walking backward toward me, just up the road, round the next bend, over the rise, our faces facing each other only once we've passed each other by, after which and just before she disappears from view I might call out, "Look for me under your boot soles. That's where I'll look for you."

NOW I LAY ME

because if I don't, at my age, who will?
And anyway, it's only the first nights
that I was really good at, that I miss,

or even earlier before the first kiss:
cock's man of expectation, I had a gift,
a calling, or, at least, was on call for

the accidental come-on of a hand
that brushes hand too often or too long
to be mistaken for an accident,

touch taut with possibility, with thrill
so fresh it's still a facet of the fear
it might not happen and the hope it will,

button by fumbled button, holding back
to make the later rushing forward even faster,
and all the pillow talk before and after,

stories of exes, stories of love disasters
inflicted or endured, all angled now
with insight and compassion never felt

before, in which the ugliest of errors,
because confessed to so unflinchingly,
transforms the teller into what each finds

so irresistible about the other,
and never mind the stories that are theirs
alone, that follow every kabbalistic

twist of happenstance, which in the telling
had to have happened so that this could happen,
which only makes their having met at all

seem both predestined and impossible.
Because my better half was the half imagined,
the half suspended out of breath arriving,

the loose gowns go on falling from the shoulders
of the bodies that have never finished falling
to the sheets beneath them still as smooth as snow

inside me falling in a white amnesia
over breath, thigh, lip, and fingertip:
Whose is it? Does it even matter now,

or did it ever, for the sky has cleared
and the white ice of moonlight fills the bed
on these long last nights when I lay me down?

Four

LETTERS

1.

I never saw the rabbi's face, only the dusty rumpled black suit in
the ground floor open window, the skull-capped head bent over a
massive tome of pages so thin you could see through them when a
crooked finger turned one over, the print on both sides for a second
visible, like a cloud of gnats in sunlight; always in the other hand a
black pointer I didn't know was called a yad, whose gold tip shaped
like a pointing finger glided trembling right to left across the words
he mumbled along to, chanting Ha Shem this and Ha Shem that.
Morning and evening, I saw him there, bent over reading, reading,
reading, chained by his own hand to the yad that pulled the hand
across and down page after page until to my unimportant unnotice-
able comings and goings, who knows where or for what, too small
to matter, never expected to matter, I must have thought he prayed
to Ha Shem to release him from that ball and chain of reading,
from every half-sighed Ha Shem that told me he was sorry, he was
truly sorry, for whatever bad thing he had done.

2.

Then one day I was made to stand before the letters that spelled
my name on the kindergarten wall, next to the names of kids
standing in front of theirs. The letters were the sound of who I was
when nobody was saying them. They would say them even if no
one listened. Even when I was gone. It was like looking at a mirror
that reflected my self back at me from some entirely unknown
dimension. It was stranger than the mirror my parents' bed backed
up against, than seeing not just my body but what was behind and

to either side of it, reversed and multiplied, the television on a low shelf to my right now to my left inside the mirror, where another smaller version of me stood inside another version of the room, looking out from what was looking in. My name, what made me me, became a jigsaw puzzle made of sound pieces you had to fit sight pieces to, but no sooner had you fitted this piece to that than they themselves would break apart into smaller pieces, and still smaller till there was no way to know if they were adding up to or subtracting from the big picture I was there to make out of the letters of my name.

3.

Suddenly there were compacts, expectations, understandings I could not undo. I knew the sound of all the English letters but not all the shapes. And beyond the shapes I did and didn't know, there were all these pages full of clumps of letters, screes of letters, deep dark forests, hilly countrysides and continents of words I would have to cross to get to where everyone my age was going, where everybody older expected us to go. Suddenly it would be shameful not to. Whatever I had been before, whomever I thought I was was now of no account; it wasn't adorable or precious to misspeak. It wasn't cute to make up the words I pretended to be reading. I had taken the wrong train or had stepped off at the wrong station full of people I knew but who now knew me as someone else, someone they insisted had to live here in this new land they called "OR ELSE," because, if there were any privileges, favors, and affections to be gotten, Mister, this was how you got them. OR ELSE.

4.

And there were sheets of pages too, and each sheet was lined. The crayon, the pencil, the pen became a kind of yad, a yad that wrote down letters, that insisted that the letters stay between the lines, so big and no bigger, so small and no smaller: the ordinary letters were to capitals as we were to grown-ups. But even the small ones had to stand straight, look sharp, not wiggle. There had to be so much space, no more, no less, between the letters that made the words, and a little more but not too much between the words that made the sentences. There was nothing you could do now that wouldn't be corrected.

5.

In a schoolhouse at the foot of a mountain in a faraway land: on the first day of school, the teacher leads the youngest children up the mountain, up a winding path through fields, meadows, forests, higher and higher past the shrinking trees, above the tree line to a stony wind-swept summit—too far above the village for the rules to reach, beyond the reach of grown-ups, parents, even teachers, she tells the children to shout out into the wind whatever they want, whatever they're not allowed to say or think below, their secret names, the words they dare not share with others, forbidden words, nonsense words, the baby talk they're too big to speak now but too small not to want to, just this once and never again she has them shout it all out into the wind that carries it away across the unlined white paper of the clouds before she leads them back down the mountain to the schoolhouse where they must learn the local habitation and a name she has prepared for each and every one of them.

6.

Each of the five identical Chinese brothers had a special power— one could drink up the sea, another had a neck of iron; fire couldn't burn the third; the fourth could stretch his legs like taffy, and the fifth could hold his breath forever. Miss Cunningham paused after reading every page and held the book up for us to see the first brother, a fisherman (head swollen like a giant balloon), spit the sea out that drowns the child, that condemns the fisherman to death, first by hanging, then by drowning, then by burning, and then by suffocation, but as each brother secretly takes the place of the brother before him, no one is hanged, drowned, burned, or suffocated, and the fisherman is freed. But it's the last brother I couldn't for some reason stop thinking about long after story hour was over and we were lying on our mats for naptime in the now dark, silent room: how they put him like a pizza or a loaf of bread on a wide, flat wooden shovel called a peel and slid him into the low, airless oven and slammed shut the door. When they released him next morning he rubbed his eyes a little, smiling, yawning, stretching, as from a good night's sleep, but he couldn't have slept inside that cramped black space in which eyes closed or open you saw the same unbroken unbreakable blackness; holding your breath all night you wouldn't have even heard the breathing sounds that thickened around me as everybody napped, and after blackness such as that even the smallest bit of daylight would have stung the eyes, would have been a blinding in itself.

7.

The universe inflated. Or, small as I was, I shrunk.

8.

In a later page of the book of life, I'd learn the suit that hung down all the way to their ankles like a dress was called a *changshan*; the skullcap that was so like the rabbi's was called a *baikal*. And even later that the pigtail was like the Yellow Star the rabbi as a young man had been forced to wear. I'd learn the oven was like an oven.

9.

We were all in the book of life reading books while God read us.
God held a holy yad and read the words of what our every moment
couldn't help but be, from one end of the story to the other. And in
the meantime if you know what's good for you, Mister, you don't
gawk at the rabbi. After what he's been through, you don't point.
You don't laugh. Don't talk about him. Don't ask me about him.
When you're older, maybe. Just be a big boy. Pretend he isn't there.

10.

If you stood too close to the poster of the painting on the bulletin
board beside the teacher's desk you couldn't see the picture; you saw
what the TV looked like before the cartoons came on early Sunday
morning; you had to step away, move back to where the desks were,
before the paint would stir and ripple into windy grass, trees, and
water. You had to hold the book just so far from your eyes too, no
farther, for the words to be words and not squid and jellyfish adrift
in underwater whiteness. You couldn't forget it was the paint that
made you think it wasn't paint even while it reminded you it was.
Terrible things went on almost happening in the books we read. To
see what was in them we had to hold them from us. But the words
didn't care one way or the other; they weren't alive even while the
living almost died inside them. The bent grass and rippling water
made visible the wind you couldn't see. What infused life and went
on living was not alive. Even now the brother is being slid into an
oven. Is being guillotined. Drowned. Burned. Suffocated. Even
now only the stupid kid is dead. Which serves him right because
he didn't come when called. If you don't die you must be innocent.
Too bad the rabbi doesn't know that, doesn't realize he's nowhere to
be found. That's why I've brought him back and chained him to the
yad and book where he must beg Ha Shem for forgiveness from the
very words it is his punishment to have to read.

HOLOCENE

One afternoon during a rainstorm
in what was still the Holocene,
although I didn't know this then,
I thumbed through a picture book
called *Deep Time* whose first
blank page it said was outer space
before anything existed
to be the outer of, and whose
last page titled "dawn of man"
was just a red hand on a cave wall—
splayed ochre thumb and fingers
and a palm the size of mine
pressed up it almost seemed
from deep inside the stone
as if to push free of the stone
and page into the dim-lit
cave-like air I breathed
inside the school I'd run into
for cover when the rain began.

I held my hand up, palm out,
palm to palm, as if to greet it,
but what I felt was just how thin
the page was, just a phantom
membrane between hand and hand,
and book and air; the nothing
of it passed right through me

into depths that hadn't been there
till it got inside and made
the pages flicker between
my fingers in a motion picture
of the nothing I could otherwise
not see: stone ran like water;
mountain melted into forest
into veld that ice floes ebbed
and flowed across; entire continents
like combers broke and pounded
onto one another, up
and over endlessly on and on.

The rain kept falling. The schoolyard
asphalt pocked with puddles
down below me quivered
as if about to break apart
from what seemed to be reaching up
from deep inside it, all across it, bits
and pieces of tall trees pitching
and bucking upside down
above an under sky the falling
rain was also rising from.
Someone over someone else
went running sole to sole
across the healed as soon as shattered
two-way mirror that the outside was.
And then the storm got darker.
And for a moment I was looking
through the specter of my looking
till the clouds broke, and the day brightened,
and in the sudden glitter I was gone.

AT THE MUSEUM OF LIFE AND SCIENCE

In the first room there was a room-sized, floor-
to-ceiling, Rube Goldberg chain reaction
domino contraption, a thicket dense
with consequence, constructed out of ramps,
gates, doorways, trapdoors, holes, and balls you set
sequentially in motion when you pulled a cord,
and on the highest ramp a gate went up,
and a ball slightly bigger than a marble
rolled down a zigzag rampart off a ledge
into a bucket that the weight of the ball dropped
by pulley to a lower ledge that tipped the bucket
over so that the ball spilled out and tumbled
down a chute onto a switch it flipped,
which sprung a spring inside a nearby hole
from which another ball popped out and rolled
onto a steeply undulating ramp
whose peaks and troughs were pitched just so, so that
the ball went only fast enough, descending
to slow without quite stopping, going up.

Each moment of it made a kind of this-
from-that coherence that the whole machine—
in all its intricately manic loop-
de-looping disconnectedness from anything
beyond itself—completely contradicted.

What you forgot about inside it waited
in the next room, which was the universe:
an all-black floor-to-ceiling emptiness
whose few stars shone so faintly under and
above and all around you that without
quite ever vanishing they seemed to shrink
away into the void to make it even
blacker and more endless than it was.

You stood in nothing, on nothing, aimless,
inconsequential, free of consequence.
So far away from anything to miss,
you couldn't think or feel enough to miss it.
Your very flesh, mind, self, what made you you
was turned there into a vacancy inside
a vacancy that had no start or finish,
no here there right left up or down,
while next door ball banged ball down ramps, up chutes,
through curving avenues and winding tunnels
in blind devotion to the force that passed
itself from ball to ball as in a race
against the counterforce the next room was,
that chased by never moving, that won by staying
fixed where it was, which now was everywhere,
inside and out, the one room in the other,
even in daylight, from the museum stairs,
in traffic inching past from both directions,
stopping and starting perfectly in sync,
until a bus pulled out of it up to
a bus stop where, like clockwork, bodies from

within themselves were choosing what outside
themselves was where they couldn't help but go
as they filed in through front doors sliding open
while other bodies filed out through the side,
and then the inching traffic as it stopped
and started opened for the bus and closed
around it, carrying it away the way
the sidewalk carried away the bodies mingling,
swerving, in all directions, peeling off.

TEN STATEMENTS OF NOT KNOWING

1.   The elements that compose the chemicals
     that make the cells that constitute my life,
     that keep me living, aren't themselves alive.

2.   Almost all of what my body does
     it does without my knowing anything
     about it; without any sense of me
     involved, including how the unalive
     electro-chemical circuits of the I
     that's thinking this is even thinking this.

3.   As if the feeling of I-am inheres
     in the not knowing how it is I am.

4.   It's like my brain's been put (by whom?
     by what?) in a blind trust whose holdings
     and how they're being handled I can't know
     even while what I do know, think, and feel
     depends on and exists through what I can't.

5.   Outside a bird is singing in the trees,
     and my fingers move so swiftly over the keys
     to type "outside a bird is singing in the trees"
     that it's my fingers not my ears that think
     they hear it asking, "What did it mean?
     What did it mean? What did it mean?"

6. It is my fingers, not my eyes,
   that see the dog beneath the trees look up
   and tilt his head as if he's asking too.

7. At the brain's bidding, if we can call it that,
   specific muscles in the dog's neck contract,
   cocking the head sideways into a question mark.

8. The brain has even less of an idea
   of how it does this than my fingers know
   about the brain that tells them what to type.

9. Routines are made of subroutines that sub-
   routines compose from top to bottom, substrate
   to superstructure network overlaid
   on network node to flashing node reworked,
   repurposed to a ghostly juggling act

10. of thinking I'm awake, aware, choosing
    to write this, not that, attend to this, not that,
    because, hey you, it's me, you know me, don't you,
    the guy who types "a bird is singing from the trees,"
    and as it sings for reasons of its own,
    is unaware, like me, of how it sings,
    or if the dog's head tilted might be hearing
    what I can almost think the bird is saying
    until it's said it, and the dog stops listening,
    and dog and bird together wander off
    out of the words that go on wondering
    what any of it means or might have meant.

ART ACCORDING TO CURLY

He never learns.
When brother Moe
holds a fist out
saying hit this,
he hits it, and surprise!
the fist wheels round
to bop him
on his own head—
over and over,
and all this while
the world is after him,
on the run from cop,
landlord, boss, or wife
until he ducks
into a fancy
kitchen, and donning
apron and chef
hat white as the
flour he dumps
on the counter, as the paint
he mistakes the milk
for and the salt
he thinks is sugar
while he kneads it all
together up to his

elbows in it,
he can't help but sing;
he's singing in that
La-Li la-la la-li
la-la falsetto

paradise of his own
making that makes
nothing useful
aping use—and
when the boss
the wife the cop
the real chef
blow by him through
the kitchen as even
brother Moe
blows by enraged
and blaming him
for everything, it's like
he can't be seen,
he can't be touched,
as if the singing
walled off the body
that otherwise
is just the bull's
eye of every hurt
conceivable, a singing
slapstick shield
of Achilles that
protects only
the shield maker

and only while
the shield is
being made—
with glittery bitch
slap on this panel
and bright eye
gouge on that
and in the middle
a cake the muckety-
mucks gag on,
and the jig
is up, and there
he is running
in place beside
a bronze Moe
holding a bronze
fist out saying
hit this, and every
time he does.

TEN THOUGHTS ON TRAUMA AND CATHARSIS

1. Trauma is the thought balloon around the flickering ellipsis of a text that never comes because it's never ending on a back-lit screen of the mobile device catharsis thinks it is.

2. All the options to undo, repeat, clear, select all, paste, find, and copy always appear on the edit menu of the new document page Catharsis promises to Trauma, but only as washed-out autistic apparitions that don't change or move when clicked on.

3. Catharsis mistakes a belly flop for a swan dive into a tar pit Trauma butterflies across.

4. Over and over Trauma turns to the bottle that for Catharsis is a draft of Aristotle.

5. Guess who says: my mantra's motto's mojo's doh jo's MO is "release."

6. Guess who hears "releash."

7. The reward center of the subject's brain lights up at random intervals but only frequently enough to keep the flickering ever-just-about-to-be-extinguished hope from ever quite going out. Catharsis is the tag, the like, the post or comment, the cryptic message out of the blue on Trauma's Facebook page so Trauma (just as it's about to) can't stop scrolling, scrolling, scrolling for any passing mention of its name.

8. In the middle of an orgasm the mangled faces of Trauma and Catharsis can't be told apart except for the eyes—the shocked wide-open not-you-again eyes of the one staring straight up into the squeezed-shut see-no-evil eyes of the other.

9. Trauma is a germ, a fungus, impervious to medication in the prone Panglossian body of Catharsis: proliferating even posthumously until everything tests positive, walls, bed, doors, curtains, phones, sink, soap, poles, pump, window shades, ceiling, and floor tiles that need now to be ripped out and replaced in this best of all possible rooms.

10. Up through collapsed, turned-inside-out interiors, broken architraves, and shattered windows, the Three Dog Night ringtone of a cellphone in a pinned hand goes on singing "Joy to the World," and despite themselves, all the boys and girls are singing too, the fishes in the deep blue sea, and you and me, they sing, and won't stop singing just as long as nobody, not Trauma, or Catharsis, ever picks up.

PASTIME

About as useful as a pitch-black hall of mirrors
or an iWatch in eternity, with Siri saying "Sorry,
I missed that" to nobody in particular,
all the personal data dormant, moot, mute—

mornings, back when the work was new,
with my coffee and the white page, and the whole day
ahead of me without distraction, I'd play

my go-to pastime imagining the old man I would be
four decades later in the same chair
at the same desk imagining his younger self
imagining his older.
                                    You blind deaf dumb

phantasmagoria, was this your idea
of being funny? Was I your pastime?
What in the world have you done with me?

HAZEL

My cluelessness, which not surprisingly
I'm unaware of, goes by the name of
Hazel, a girl I knew
in college whom I haven't thought of since then
and to be honest never much thought of
then, and even now
I couldn't say for sure
if the face I picture
looks anything like her face.

Why was she just so, I don't know, so
always just around, so
nondescript, so neither
fat nor thin, but like
she might have once been
either, companionably
inoffensive and ignorable? Why did her laughter,
peculiarly her own,
the sneezy hand-on-mouth

ah-chew of it, seem at once
too shy and frequent, too demur
and eager, like the white noise
of a sitcom laugh track
you'd only notice
if it wasn't there?

Would it amuse her
that I learned on Facebook
from a friend I also don't remember

that she died twenty years ago
today, at forty-seven, and that from the picture
(was it the last?),
despite the shriveled figure,
bald head too gaunt to bother
covering with a scarf,
a teenage daughter lying
by her side, a grown son
behind the bed, his hands

on her shoulders, her hands on his,
though nearly nothing,
she was still laughing—she
who had been, it seemed,
for me alone
the face of nothing,
was laughing—but at me
now, me, the joke I am,
the joke I never got?

O my ranks on ranks of Hazels,
my supporting casts,
my paparazzi
of a heartlessness unseen,
unheard behind the flashing cameras
I still mug for, late as it is

and all alone, in the same old
scene I steal, how could you not
be laughing, jeering

at this rachitic aging diva
in high heels
on a subway grate a hot wind
is blowing up through
into this skirt I'm struggling
to hold down over
private parts so
bald now like a baby's
you would never guess they once had hair?

GRAVITY AND GRACE

Gravity is odorless as God, and like God is everywhere, invisible and weightless, inside and between what in its absence could have no inside or between, no mass or form to get free or give in to it with.

In a vacuum there is no falling, or if there is, because everything big and small is falling at the same speed, at the same time, you can't tell falling from floating.

In hospice, my father cried like a baby in a wet crib, eyes shut, inconsolable, because I couldn't be his mother, or, if I could, could only be the sleep-deprived postpartum mother who can't lift her massive body from the quicksand of exhaustion, too sunk in heaviness to do anything about what by then she only wanted to be rid of, whispering shhh, shhh, shhh to his runaway accelerating O O Os as if to slow them to a canter, a trot, a standstill,

and when his heart stopped and the busily communicating cells inside the hand that held mine forgot what they were saying, or that they were even cells, or that the hand had ever been a hand, unballing its viselike fist from around my fingers, gravity

was all that held body to bed, bed to hospice, hospice to earth.

Its micro-grip tightened on every subatomic bit of every particle there was, on everything I had pretended right up to then it wasn't pulling down.

When I stood up my father was the force I stood up against. Invisible and weightless as the piss stink rising from the bed, which like a baby he had wet, the inside of his thighs were rash red, his grizzled ball sack even redder between the scorched white pubic hairs.

Only once the odor had spread everywhere and covered everything could you not smell it. Not smelling it was grace, which is the opposite of gravity, from which there's no escape.

HOLE IN ONE

Since my dad was blind by then,
when David and I led him from his apartment
to the tee of the shrunken one-hole
golf course that served as kitschy
courtyard for the complex
of retirees only well-off
enough for this unironic
aping of the rich, it was by habit
only that he looked down
at the ball he couldn't see,
then up and out into the void
of stunted fairway and green
while first this foot then that
foot patted the fake grass, almost
kneading it catlike till the tight
swing arced the ball up high

as the second-story windows,
and I swear it was like a trick
ball the pin on an invisible line
reeled in straight down
into the hole—his first and only
hole in one, on the last swing
of a club he ever took, though
we didn't know this then, and how
we whooped, my brother and I,

as we jumped and capered, throwing
the other balls up into the air
while the old man, baffled, said, "What?
what happened? What?" already wistful
for this best moment of a life it was
his luck the blindness made him miss.

And now it's my luck, isn't it just
my luck, to be the last one
remembering, as if I'm not just
there with them but also far
removed above it all and watching
as through the block glass of an upper-story
window high enough for the ruckus
not to reach me but too low
not to see the filmy blur of
bodies hugging one another,
pumping fists as arm-in-arm
the three of them head out across
the fake grass of that one last hole.

TREE ON MOUNTAIN

Nat and Izzy had climbed ahead of me, turning
and calling to make sure I was still behind them;
"Come on old man," they shouted. Too winded to laugh,

I looked up, and wind stung my view of them
to water, all the way up past bogland
greenly darkening spongelike underfoot,

up past washed-out clumps of gorse and lousewort
and impossible-to-pinpoint sounds of trickling
as I kept climbing to my grown kids

into wind past any hint of soil
or water to where even the toughest lichen gave way
to moonscape, while they climbed higher,

calling after me, "Come on Dad, we're almost there,"
rubble of quartzite everywhere, tall spikes
and slabs gray as cloud cover

I could almost touch,
my children almost lost in cloud
while underfoot cloud turned to stone—

their bodies braced against a lone
tree hard as stone
grown sideways, stunted, all its branches bent

in zigzag fractals, shaking as if trying to push
up higher against what pushed
down harder

because it hated any rising thing.
Eyes stung in the onrush even when I looked away;
everything blurred

to water, salt water of such a constant hate
that when the sun at last seeped through
a chink of cloud,

and stone and tree and cloud
and my children too all
brightened like light on water

before it all again went dark when the sky did
while the wind kept pouring over bright
and dark, it seemed just then

I'd never reach them, never hear them.
The higher I climbed the more climbing felt like sinking
to the floor of a ghost sea

while my children called "Daddy! Daddy!"
soundlessly through water
to the very bottom of it all.

THE OLD AGE OF OLIVER

I was old by the time everyone had died.
It wasn't their dying that made me old,

it was their being dead. See, I was old
once there was no one to be younger than.

I guess that's what I loved about their dying,
the way their getting closer to the end

let me feel further from it, how sitting there
upright beside their lying down

made me feel taller, freer when I'd leave,
and how by leaving I got to be the one

returning in a halo of health, angelic
with news, a kind of artful dodger

picking gold coins from the pocket
of each dying, getting away with it

at least till I became myself
the empty pocket the dead picked clean,

down to this half-
conniving hunger for the

the orphan child
of my own old age

in a noisy lunchroom asking
please sir a little more sir

of what there's no one left to give.

DEATH OF ALAN

On the old playground two lines of pallid
almost see-through silt-swirl smears

of almost faces face each other, every face
a rippling sameness, a wispy little ego clot

I think is me, my face, suspended
between what's neither aftermath nor

onset as all of them join hands to make
two chains of me, two memes of me, my

every precious irreducible smudge and tic
diminishing from one end of the playground

to the other, growing smaller now
the more me's of me there are, and every me is chanting,

"Red Rover Red Rover, send Alan right over"—
but Alan, poor Alan, seeing only Alan

everywhere, he's had it with the game, because
it never ends, the calling out and sending over,

Beth first, then David, Claudia, Wil, Charlie,
and Tom, and Mark and Tim, and who the hell is

red rover anyway? And what's he gonna do
if my hand gripped in my hand grips so tightly

there's no chance anywhere along the chain
of me's of myself ever breaking through?

GHOST STORY

I was my own ghost
even before
I learned to depend
without affection
on affection.

An almost shape
of chalk dust
at the mercy of a
drafty bedroom
where wire hangers

when I pass them
ping so singly faint
the echoes echo
for the company.
Does it even matter

who got tired
and left this book
of me half-
read, facedown
like spread wings

frozen in mid-flight
in lamplight
on the bedside table?
This vapor of an I,
this camp tale

of a dry ice
mimicry of burning
steam is made
of marks that make
the words that shout

out all at once from all
the pages pressed
so deafeningly tight
together not a single
one of them is heard.

And you, whose touch
I needed only
to more keenly
feel just how
untouchable I am,

I'd like to think
you comprehended—
later, if not then—
that I couldn't
make sense of you,

of being with you
till you couldn't bear
to turn another
page and left;
that leaving was

the only sound
I *could* hear and
could only hear it
once the long
fade-out faded

too faint to be heard.